Greater Than a 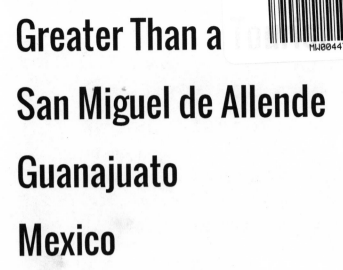 San Miguel de Allende Guanajuato Mexico

50 Travel Tips from a Local

Tom Peterson

Lock Haven, PA

ISBN: 9781521419786

DEDICATION

This book is dedicated to my parents, who taught me the value of family and friends, my grandparents, who gave me the courage and inspiration to venture to new lands, and my daughter, who reminds me to follow my dreams and passions.

BOOK DESCRIPTION

Are you excited about planning your next trip?

Do you want to try something new while traveling?

Would you like some guidance from a local?

If you answered yes to any of these questions, then this book is just for you.

Greater Than a Tourist San Miguel de Allende, Guanajuato, Mexico by Tom Peterson offers the inside scope on San Miguel de Allende. Most travel books tell you how to travel like a tourist. Although there's nothing wrong with that, as a part of the Greater than a Tourist series, this book will give you travel tips from someone who lives at your next travel destination.

In these pages you'll discover local advice that will help you throughout your stay. This book will not tell you exact addresses or store hours but instead will give you an excitement and knowledge from a local that you may not find in other smaller print travel books. Travel like a local. Slow down, stay in one place, and get to know the people and the culture of a place.

By the time you finish this book, you will be eager and prepared to travel to your next destination.

Contents

Author Bio

Tom Peterson was born in New York, New York, and grew up in that area of the northeast, until he decided it was time to start a new life in San Francisco, California, where he moved at the age of 24. During his first two years living in the Bay Area he considered new careers in landscaping, carpentry, opening an ice cream shop, a bar/restaurant, and leading unique tours of San Francisco, among other things. What he really enjoyed most were the five trips he took across America those first two years, taking a different route, vehicle, and fellow travelers on each trip.

Before long he had adventured to all 50 states in the U.S. and decided it was time to see more of the rest of the world. His careers in the airline, film, video game, and technology industries, marketing communications, internet telephony, online sports instruction, and higher education businesses, much of it in international business development, opened the door for travel to many countries around the world.

But he longed to live in another country, learn another language, and immerse himself in the culture and with the people of a land much different from the one where he grew up. Looking south to a country he always loved, but to a part of it he had never visited, he moved to San Miguel de Allende, Mexico, a 16th century colonial city in the historical heartland of the high desert mountains of central Mexico, in October 2015.

Living there and loving it for more than a year and a half, Tom felt like he had many interesting stories, and much valuable information to share, with anyone considering traveling to one of the most beautiful, extraordinary, and romantic places in the world.

HOW TO USE THIS BOOK

This book was written by someone who has lived in an area for over three months. The author has made the best suggestions based on their own experiences in the area. Please check that these places are still available before traveling to the area. The goal of this book is to help travelers either dream or experience different locations by providing opinions from a local.

FROM THE PUBLISHER

Traveling can be one of the most important moments in a person's life. The memories that you have of anticipating going somewhere new or getting to travel are some of the best. As a publisher of the Greater Than a Tourist book series, as well as the popular 50 Things to Know book series, we strive to help you learn about new places, spark your imagination, and inspire you.

Thought this book you will find something for every traveler. Wherever you are and whatever you do I wish you safe fun, and inspiring travel.

Lisa Rusczyk Ed. D.

CZYK Publishing

WELCOME TO > TOURIST

WHY AM I A LOCAL?

Looking for a unique international location where I would feel both at home, and very much away from home, as an expat for the first time, a friend in San Francisco mentioned San Miguel de Allende to me in February 2015. I had not only never been there, I had never even heard of the place. I had been to Mexico many times, but mostly up and down the west coast, from Baja California to Puerto Vallarta and Acapulco. Those places are not really the real Mexico, but rather the sun and surf vacationers' idea of Mexico. A few weeks later I was in San Miguel. The first day there I knew I was going to move there, a phenomenon that I came to learn over the next two years is highly common. The place is not known as a ciudad mágica for nothing. To anyone who has ever been to San Miguel no explanation is needed. For those considering visiting for the first time, I will provide a brief explanation here. San Miguel is known to attract artists, musicians, writers, and all types of creative people from all over the world. It is a combination of the multicultural, multilingual, international stew of adventurous people searching for a new life, or for some changes in an already full life, complemented with the light, the air, and the beauty of the architecture preserved mostly as it was in the 16th, 17th, and 18th centuries. Combine world class cuisine, striking and unique living environments, and some of the best climate on the planet, and you have found a place to spend the rest of your days, or just a week or a month to enhance your life.

1. Visit A Very Unique Best World City Award Location

I obviously was not reading all of the right travel magazines prior to 2015, when I first heard of San Miguel de Allende, in the state of Guanajuato, in the mountains and historical heartland of central Mexico. If I had been I would have known of this still fairly well-kept secret of a jewel much sooner. Among many other best in the world awards San Miguel de Allende (usually just referred to by locals as San Miguel) took 3rd place on Travel + Leisure's 2016 "World's Best Cities" list. With a score of 91.19 out of 100, Travel + Leisure explains how San Miguel de Allende qualified for their list: "Readers ranked cities on their sights and landmarks, culture, cuisine, friendliness, shopping, and overall value. We're looking for the whole package—history, culture, exciting cuisine, modernity, antiquity, and everything in between. It sounds like a tall order, but the world's best cities offer these attributes and more. San Miguel de Allende has seen a significant transformation in recent years... A UNESCO World Heritage site, it possesses a certain mountain-town charm that not all cities have: its friendly local feel is matched only by its energy and festivals. As one T+L voter described, 'the plaza is their living room. It's an art lover's paradise.' In addition to 3rd place on the overall World's Best Cities List, San Miguel also placed as the number one city in Mexico, Central, and South America!" Other World's Best Cities lists that San Miguel has been included on recently include those from CNN, Condé Nast Traveler, Luxury Travel, and Luxury Living magazines.

2. Live In An Ideal Climate

If you are interested in the geography and weather in San Miguel, as most travelers are when planning a trip, the municipality of San Miguel de Allende is located in the far eastern side of the state of Guanajuato. It has an average altitude of 1,870 meters (6,135 feet) above sea level. The climate in the area is mostly temperate and semi-arid, with temperatures averaging 22 °C (72 °F). Summers are moderately hot, with a rainy season that generally produces sporadic thunderstorms, similar to tropical locations like Florida and Hawaii, but without the humidity. Winters are very moderate. Moving here from the San Francisco Bay Area, and having now been through almost two full years of weather, the best comparison I can make is with the weather in Oakland, CA. For those not familiar with the Bay Area microclimates, Oakland is warmer and drier than its neighbors, San Francisco and Berkeley, because it does not get the fog from the Pacific Ocean and the Bay, and it is not as hot as the surrounding communities only 10 minutes away, because the hills keep it cooler. It has been said that Oakland has the best climate in the U.S., never humid, or too hot or too cold, and, having been to all 50 states and every major U.S. city in my travels, I believe that is true. That is almost the same climate that we have in San Miguel, except with warmer, milder evenings and mornings. As I said during all of my years living in the Bay Area, and continue to say in San Miguel, "another gorgeous day in paradise".

3. Experience Spectacular Sunsets Nightly

Having lived most of my life, prior to moving to Mexico, in the New York City metropolitan area and the San Francisco Bay Area of California, I was never more than a short drive away from an ocean and a beach, and loved seeing sunrises and sunsets (mainly sunsets, my favorite time of the day) over the water. I knew that by moving to San Miguel I would be giving up my close proximity to the ocean, but an expected delight has been the spectacular sunsets, on a nightly basis, from any rooftop in San Miguel, and even out my bedroom window at home.

Since the large lake in the area, La Presa, lies to the west of the city, and there are no tall buildings in San Miguel, the routinely enchanting sunsets can be seen from almost anywhere, usually going down over the water.

4. Immerse Totally: Mexican Living, Spanish Language

The most popular Spanish language school in San Miguel is the Warren Hardy School. It has been here for over 25 years and more than 10,000 students have attended it. Since San Miguel is a community with many part-time residents, with thousands of Americans and Canadians spending anywhere from a month to six months every year here, the "part-time" schools cater to the part time and full time residents looking to improve their Spanish. But for those wishing to take a deeper dive there are total immersion schools offering classes here as well. These schools help you find living accommodations with Mexican families, who speak no English, so you are forced to speak Spanish all of the time around the house. The classes are often five days a week, eight hours a day, with no English spoken in the classroom either. These classes tend to be filled with a higher percentage of younger students, from high schools and universities, or who are in the early stages of their careers.

5. Pick Up La Atencion/Que Pasa: Events In San Miguel

When I first visited San Miguel in 2015 I was told "Everything that is going on in San Miguel is in 'La Atencion'." "La Atencion" is a weekly bilingual newspaper, sold every Friday, containing stories of local interest, highlights of upcoming fiestas and special events, and an insert section called "Que Pasa" that provides a calendar of events for the next two week period, in both Spanish and English. It is the weekly "bible" of San Miguel happenings, and most people I know buy it religiously each Friday. However, I learned pretty quickly that not *every* event going on in San Miguel is contained within its covers. In fact, I estimate that at most it is somewhere between 10-20% of the events, and mostly events that repeat each week. So much that happens in San Miguel is communicated by word of mouth and, with a growing younger and more tech savvy population, through Facebook and other social media outlets. Another resource that I have found to be very useful in learning about events, and for the excellent articles about San Miguel people, places, and things, is "San Miguel Events", found online at *sanmiguelevents.com*. A few other places to find out about events in San Miguel are: *thascenesanmiguel.com*, *sanmiguelliterarysala.org*, *atencionsanmiguel.org*, and the "Civil List", a San Miguel Yahoo! group where anyone who signs up (you do not have to be a resident) can ask any San Miguel-related questions of the group.

6. Watch Your Step: Colorful Buildings And Cobblestone Streets

The buildings and streets of San Miguel are as magical as so many other things in this magic town. In the historic center, there are an estimated two thousand doors, behind which there are at least two thousand courtyards of various sizes. Many of these have been restored to their former colonial state, with façades of deep red, brown, maroon, ochre, orange and yellow, windows and doors framed by handcrafted ironwork and made of hewn wood. Very few structures have atriums or front yards; instead, open private space is behind the main façade in courtyards. The town is noted for its streetscapes, with narrow cobblestone lanes that rise and fall over the hilly terrain, and occasionally defy colonial attempts to make a straight grid. It is still a small city, and at night, many wander the narrow streets. But watch your step, day or night: San Miguel is not known as "The City Of Fallen Women" for nothing. The narrow sidewalks, uneven cobblestone streets, and plethora of interesting sights to look at while you are walking inevitably lead to tumbling walkers. And I know from personal experience, and from that of many of my guy friends, that it is not only the women who have fallen! The people on the streets are a mix of Mexicans, foreigners, and indigenous. A key part of the diverse makeup of the city, very different from in the United States or Europe, is that the original indigenous peoples, the Otomis and Nahuas (Chichimecas), can be seen on the streets, as they come from their rural communities to sell and buy goods, as well as to attend church.

7. Glide Past The Doors Of San Miguel

I had a poster that I loved from Ireland, home of my ancestors and many relatives, called "The Doors of Ireland". Until I arrived in San Miguel I was never more fascinated with doors than those I witnessed in the Emerald Isle. But walking through the colonial center of San Miguel de Allende, and paying attention to the doors of the buildings, is like a daily free tour of a unique living museum.

The doors themselves can range in size from as small as four feet high and three feet wide, an entrance way that my five year old self, or Tyrion Lannister, the dwarf from "Game of Thrones", would feel comfortable walking through, to 12 foot high and equally wide monstrosities that an NBA center, or, possibly, Wun Weg Wun Dar Wun, the wildling giant from "Game of Thrones", might be able to duck his way through. Beyond sheer size, there are the variations in the types and ages of the materials the doors are made from and, more impressively, the door handles. Bears, lions, snakes, eagles, rings of all types, anything goes when it comes to what you will grab ahold of when entering a home or place of business.

Yet, as thrilling as the doors can be, my favorite part is the world of surprise awaiting the opening of those doors. Behind each one could be a small studio apartment or, more likely, a whole new world you never imagined all of the times you previously walked by them. One usually assumes when entering the front door of a home elsewhere that you will go into the living room, or at least a foyer leading directly into a room where indoor living takes place. Not so in colonial San Miguel. You might walk into an area with huge trees, plants, lawns, flowers, fountains, sculptures, surrounded by five or more different residences, or one massive single family home the size of a grand hacienda, with four or five levels going back to the next street and reaching up to the stars.

8. Roam The Streets Of A World Class Walking City

Speaking of walking past the doors of San Miguel, if there is a better small walking city in the world (I am not counting great, large walking cities like Paris, Rome, or New York) I have yet to find it. In almost two years of daily walking I have yet to grow tired of the never-ending array of visual stimulation. The *calles* of this town are enthralling! The buildings, sidewalks, cobblestone streets, mountains, sky, and high desert flora are light-years beyond ample.

On top of that are the always captivating wide open shops, the art galleries, music in the streets, free and independent dogs, and the most intriguing looking people, from their clothes to whatever they are carrying or doing. It is simply little wonder that people can retire to San Miguel for the rest of their lives and never be bored.

9. Cruise Town In Little Green Taxis

I have loved driving throughout most of my life, having driven across the U.S. many times, and all over the world, including on the "wrong" side of the car and the "wrong" side of the road, in England, Ireland, Australia, and the Caribbean. But after visiting San Miguel and seeing what a great walking city it is, and how many expats live there without a car, I decided to sell mine in California when I moved to San Miguel. What made that decision, and the joy of living here car-less, much easier is the proliferation of green taxis everywhere in San Miguel. No matter where I am in town, or when, it always seems there is a passenger-free taxi coming by within a few minutes at most. Except, as in most cities in the world, when it is raining! The good news is that it rarely rains in San Miguel. I asked my driver the other day, in my still improving Spanish, how many green taxis are there in San Miguel. He told me: "400 in total, with 400 driving around in the mornings, 300 in the afternoons, and 200 in the evenings." Whatever the numbers, they have it figured out, because the system works very well. And, a bonus for more luxury auto and tech-minded travelers: Uber came to San Miguel in August 2016.

10. Tour The Colonias Of San Miguel

It took me a while to get used to calling the different areas of San Miguel *colonias*, rather than neighborhoods. I first lived on the outskirts of town, in a *casita*, a small cottage or apartment, on the grounds of a big beautiful hacienda, three miles outside of the center of town in an area known as Cieneguita. As much as I liked it there I wanted to live close to Centro Historico, so that I could walk everywhere in town, and did not have to rely upon buses, taxis, or other people's cars. After a month living outside of town a friend found me a nice home in one of the most desirable parts of San Miguel, Colonia Guadiana. It has perhaps the most attractive neighborhood park in the city, is relatively quiet, and has a highly diverse neighborhood feel to it. I learned later that it is the smallest of the 25-30 colonias in San Miguel. The area across The Ancha that closely borders Guadiana, Colonia San Antonio, is the largest, and possibly most diverse, of all of the colonias. Along its eastern border is the thriving Ancha commercial area written about in a different chapter. When you ask someone what colonia they live in the answer will give you a better idea of what their lifestyle in San Miguel may be like. They may spend a lot more time out in the country, only coming into town on their four-wheeler quad vehicle once a week or so. Conversely, they may eat every meal in one of the many fine restaurants in San Miguel, walking to every one of them, and having drinks out each night. For some who are living in a luxurious home they may rarely leave it, whereas for others home is just where they lay their head down at night after a full day of taking in everything their beautiful town has to offer.

"Thunder rumbles ... The bells of the Parroquia jangle. Blackbirds fly away in jagged triangles. People scurry under the archways of the buildings surrounding the Jardin. The shoeshine men put away their rags. The fruit woman pushes her children under her rain tarp. Mariachis pile into trucks ... The square is suddenly empty ... Large drops of rain begin to fall ...

"Pamela Alma Bass ("Mexican Rain")

11. Prepare Fresh Affordable Organic Food Daily

A lifelong friend of mine spent a year living in Perugia, Italy, so he could improve his Italian, the childhood language of both of his Italian parents. He told me then about how he loved buying all of his groceries fresh, to cook at home, on a daily basis. He ate none of the processed and frozen foods that so many Americans ate at home. I always loved that idea, but did not fully embrace it until I moved to Mexico. In San Miguel, partly because of the surrounding farming communities, and partly because of the expats who want to eat more healthily, and know that it is more affordable to do so in Mexico, there is a wonderful and wide selection of organic fruits, vegetables, and almost every kind of locally grown and raised food imaginable. I walk to the markets and stores to buy my food on a regular basis. I have not bought or eaten any frozen or processed foods in a year and a half of living in Mexico. Big bonus: I lost 25 pounds when I first moved here, and have not gained it back, even though I eat and drink whatever I want.

12. Devour Tasty Food From San Miguel Street Vendors

When I first visited San Miguel two years ago my favorite food discovery was the high quality, very tasty, and extremely inexpensive food to be eaten on the streets of the city, from the many local street vendors. Food trucks have become very trendy over the past years in the San Francisco Bay Area where I used to live. Mexico has been way ahead of that trend for a long time, and it shows in the variety and popularity of the various choices. Many gringo visitors are reluctant to buy food on the street, but San Miguel is one of the safest places in Mexico to enjoy clean and delicious street food. The variety that can be found includes tacos, tortas, birria (a meat stew), burritos, corn on the cob (typically boiled and dusted with cheese or chili powder), and, for dessert, hand-churned ice cream, with some flavors seen nowhere else, like tuna, tamarind, and tequila, or churros.

One of the best food stand locales is on the corner of Canal and Mesones, where you can find excellent tacos al pastor, a dish developed in central Mexico, brought here by Lebanese immigrants. Spicy marinated pork is skewered onto a large vertical rotisserie, then sliced to order from the spit and served with pineapple and grilled onions. I usually order three of them, although I could easily eat more.

Another tasty spot is on what many call "taco corner", on the corner of the Ancha and Nemesio Diez. Various vendors park their mobile kitchens here throughout the day, but the one I frequent the most seems to start around 7:00 PM. Their tacos come with a choice of arrachera (skirt steak), beef, chorizo (Mexican sausage), chicken, or pork. At the same corner is a fragrant flower vendor selling freshly cut lilies, daffodils, sunflowers and carnations. It amuses me when I walk by see and a lively scene around the two large taco stands, with many people seated on their portable stools and picnic tables, and think that they have as many or more customers than the finest restaurants in town.

13. Dive Into Mercados: Everything Under The Sun, And Orange Donuts Too!

American flea markets can be fun and have become a well-established institution. But they have nothing on Mexican markets, the beloved *mercados.* In San Miguel they come in all sizes and varieties. The Artisan Market is open daily and is a short walk from the center of town. There are two parts to this giant market. The indoor section is filled with a colorful variety of fruits, vegetables, flowers, and many local food specialties. The outdoor portion is a seemingly endless walk, through a narrow section of San Miguel, loaded with handcrafted items from jewelry to ceramics to stand-up mirrors, paintings, pottery and uniquely Mexican religious and spiritual gifts like *Catrinas* and *Calacas,* used to decorate the home and to celebrate the many Mexican holidays like *Dia de los Muertos* and *Semana Santa.* The Tuesday weekly market, *Tianguis de los Martes,* is the most uniquely Mexican of the markets, a guaranteed mind-blowing experience for anyone from north of the border. Anything and everything can be found for sale there, but it tends to be items more suited for everyday use, such as clothes and shoes, rather than gift items.

My personal favorite is the Saturday Organic Market. There are many products, but it is primarily for food cooked on the premises for breakfast and lunch, and organic food to take home. I try a variety of dishes each week, but my standard "dessert" is the excellent cappuccino and the orgasmic orange donuts! The finest aspect, though, is that it is the best community gathering place each week for members from every community in San Miguel. Each week I see my best friends and acquaintances, and meet new people from all over the world. And the people who gather in San Miguel tend to be some of the most interesting people you will ever meet anywhere.

14. Escape From Chain Restaurants And Stores

You can easily notice the welcome absence of traffic lights, stop signs, billboards, and street lamps in San Miguel. What did not really catch my attention until Day 8 of my eight day first visit was the even more welcome lack of chain restaurants and stores in San Miguel. Few things irk me more when I am traveling internationally than seeing a McDonald's in the middle of Paris, Beijing, or Rio. It was not until the afternoon of our last day, returning from the La Grita hot springs and walking up Canal St., that we noticed for the first time, in a building we had walked by a number of times before, the Starbucks, on one of the main corners in the historic heart of the city. The reason we had not noticed it before was that it was in such a beautiful, classic, colonial building, which blended in with the surrounding structures, and the sign was very subtle and high off of the street. Because all of the employees are friendly young Mexicans who like their jobs, and it is frequented as much by Mexicans as by foreigners, it has become an accepted part of the community. But there are plenty of expats who prefer to frequent local Mexican cafes. And, thankfully, McDonald's was consistently turned away after frequent attempts at infiltration over the years!

15. Engage In Cross – Cultural Communication: Juan's And Hank's

There is no truth to the gossip and rumors you hear, from both Mexicans and foreigners, that San Miguel is "all gringos" and a "city of expats." I have to find myself correcting those false assumptions and letting people know that San Miguel's inhabitants, despite recent growth numbers, are still more than 90% Mexican, in a city of roughly 100,000 people, *mas o menos*, depending upon how much of the outlying areas are included, and what time of year the census was taken. However, if you were to walk into either Juan's Café, one of the most popular places for coffee, breakfast, lunch, and buying CDs and DVDs in town, or Hank's Restaurante, popular for lunch and dinner, and also for their 2 for 1 happy hour drinks every day from 5:00PM until 8:00 PM (when the playing of ZZ Top's "La Grange" signals last call for happy hour each evening), you might get the impression that there are a lot more gringos in San Miguel than there actually are. But the truth is, from many hours spent in each place, like many of the most frequented and fun places in town, there is usually a very good mixture of locals and transplants, and always interesting and fascinating cross-cultural communication taking place.

16. Crash A Bohemian Hippie Enclave In Mexico

Since San Miguel is such an artistic and creative town, with a left-leaning liberal majority in the expat population, many of whom are old bohemian beatniks and hippies from the 50s, 60s, and 70s, it surprised me somewhat to find out that Guanajuato, the state in which San Miguel resides, is the most conservative of the 32 Mexican states. Yes, Mexico is a very Catholic country, and 96% of the Mexican San Miguel population is Catholic. Yet the big cosmopolitan cities of Mexico City, Guadalajara, Monterrey, and Puebla are very modern, and as influenced by current styles in fashion, music, and films as anywhere. The conservatism, it seems to me, has more to do with family, religion, and the deep love of the culture and traditions, than with political conservatism. When Donald Trump became president of the U.S. in January 2017 there were concerns among expats about how the locals would think and treat us, given all of Trump's anti-Mexico rhetoric. In my opinion it has actually brought the Mexican and expat community even closer together. Whenever I wear my 'Unidos en Amistad' ('United in Friendship') t-shirt, with its side by side Mexican and American flags, made in response to Trump's hostile comments about Mexico, everywhere around San Miguel and other parts of Mexico, I get big smiles and high fives from the locals.

17. Observe Mexican Culture's Foreign Influence

"Stirling Dickinson is without doubt the person most responsible for San Miguel de Allende becoming an international art center," says John Virtue, author of "Model American Abroad", a biography of Dickinson. Although only an amateur painter himself, Dickinson became co-founder and director of the Escuela Universitaria de Bellas Artes, an art institute that he opened in a former convent only a few months after his arrival in 1939. Due to its growth as a tourist destination, some of the most obvious culture seen on the streets of the town relates to visitors, both foreign and Mexican. To cater to the expats, retirees, and a growing, younger population of professionals, who work remotely using the internet for communications, and to the year-round population of foreign and Mexican visitors, the town contains organic cafes, boutiques, art galleries, upscale restaurants and hotels, and a wide variety of bars and nightclubs. The expat population has also done a very impressive job of giving back to the community in a variety of ways.

18. Contribute In Culture Of Giving: The NGO Community

Whenever I hear some less-informed people talk about expats taking advantage of the lower cost of living in Mexico, or not respecting the Mexican people and their culture, one of the things I inform them about is the wonderful culture of giving back to the community that has been created by the expats living in San Miguel. As mentioned, it started with Stirling Dickinson back in the 1930s, with his well-known art school, and his not-so-well-known other selfless giving activities, such as providing thousands of pairs of shoes for local children over the years. There are currently somewhere between 100 and 200 NGOs in San Miguel, started by the international community living here, providing everything from food, education, and beds, to free classes in English, writing, and art. One of the NGO organizations whose good work I am most familiar with is "Feed the Hungry San Miguel", which is committed to improving the health and well-being of children in San Miguel de Allende by alleviating hunger through school meals, family nutrition education, and community development programs. Started in 1984, they now serve thousands of elementary school-age children and their families. "Feed the Hungry San Miguel" has built, operates and provisions kitchens attached to primary schools in 25 communities in the San Miguel municipality. Another local NGO that is doing great work in the community is the Rotary Club of San Miguel de Allende. The projects they have engaged in include fighting disease, growing local economies, providing clean water, saving mothers and children, and supporting education.

19. Marvel In The Presence Of The Parroquia

They say it is not technically a cathedral, but I still insist on calling it a cathedral. In my mind it is as grand a cathedral as my favorite cathedrals in the world: Notre Dame in Paris, St. Mark's in Venice, the Cologne Cathedral in Germany, St. Patrick's in New York, Grace Cathedral in San Francisco, St. Paul's in London, and the "almost" completed (after 133 years) Gaudi Sagrada Família, in Barcelona, Spain. La Parroquia de San Miguel Arcángel, the current parish church of San Miguel, is unique in Mexico and the emblem of the town. It has a Neo-gothic façade with two tall towers that can be seen from most parts of town, and everywhere from the hills in all entrances into San Miguel. The church was built in the 17th century with a traditional Mexican façade. The current Gothic façade was constructed in 1880 by Zeferino Gutierrez, who was an indigenous bricklayer and self-taught architect. It is said Gutierrez's inspiration came from postcards and lithographs of Gothic churches in Europe. However, the interpretation is his own, clearly more a work of imagination than a copied construction.

20. Unwind In The Jardin

In front of the Parroquia church complex is the Plaza Allende, popularly known as Jardin Principal or Main Garden, but most often referred to simply as El Jardin. It was designed in a French style, with wrought iron benches, and filled with always beautifully manicured laurel trees. In addition to the church, other important structures, such as the Ignacio Allende House, the Canal House, and the municipal palace overlook and complement the garden. But the thing I think people enjoy most about the Jardin is simply sitting on the park benches and talking, in Spanish, English or, perhaps most often, Spanglish, and folks just watching the parade of passers-by, as well as the constant stream of activity adjacent to all sides of the Jardin. I get especially amused by the sight of the children chasing the birds, and bouncing their giant inflatable pencil shaped toys off the ground and running after them when they go airborne.

"Your home is in your heart and mind's eye. It is roots grounded in place, it is wings governed by no place."

Sarahlee Lawrence

("I Read Walden Once")

21. Learn At Biblioteca, Sala Quetzal, Teatro Santa Ana

The Biblioteca Pública, or Public Library, serves in many ways as the community center for San Miguel's large foreigner population. The library was established by Helen Wale, a Canadian, who wanted to reach out to local children. It is the largest privately funded, publicly accessible library in Mexico, with the second largest English language book collection in Latin America. The library has a café, book store, the Teatro Santa Ana, the Sala Quetzal event space, sponsors tours in and out of town, and prints a bilingual newspaper. The newest addition is the Stirling Dickinson School of Art, started in 2016 by a retired American expat who taught art at the high school and university levels. When he discovered that the public schools here do not offer art classes he decided to open this school, in honor of the man who first attracted artists to San Miguel in the 1930s, and started the first art school here. The vision for this new art school, in addition to providing an opportunity for talented Mexican artists to learn and grow in their art skills and creativity, is to gain university credits while still in high school, and to earn college scholarships for their art.

22. Discover San Miguel's Art Galleries

San Miguel de Allende has long had a reputation as a haven for visual artists. Beyond the influence of Stirling Dickinson already mentioned in other chapters, since the 1950s, when Diego Rivera and David Alfaro Siqueiros worked here, it has attracted professional and amateur painters, sculptors, and printmakers to the many classes and workshops available. In addition to two major art institutions, Instituto Allende and Bellas Artes, artists and art venues can be seen in various parts of the town. Fabrica La Aurora is an old textile mill that has been converted into over 40 galleries and shops selling art, furnishings and antiques. On the streets or in the parks it is not unusual to see someone sketching people or landscapes, or selling their own work.

A favorite and quite unique and unusual art gallery is in the small village of La Cieneguita, at the Chapel of Jimmy Ray, in the Casa de Las Ranas home of San Miguel artist Anado and his partner. At least two times a year he holds an open house for the community, which is well worth checking out if you happen to be in San Miguel at the time.

23. Beam Back In Time At Instituto Allende

Institute Allende is located in an enormous complex, which the De la
Canal family originally began construction on, as a retreat
and hacienda, in 1735. In 1951, Institute Allende was converted into
an art institute. The complex is filled with various courtyards, a
private chapel with colonial era frescos, a modern art gallery, and the
Bistro Mi Casa restaurant, owned by accomplished local guitar
player Gil Gutierrez. Gil plays there many nights a week, along with
outstanding local band Media Luna. Up until recently it also housed
the very popular Saturday Organic Market, which in late 2016 moved
across and down the street into a new venue.

24. Transform Within Bellas Artes

The Centro Cultural Ignacio Ramirez, also called El Nigromante, is housed in the former Hermanas de la Concepción (Sisters of the Conception) convent. The Escuela de Bellas Artes at this location was established in 1938 by Peruvian Felipe Cossío del Pomar and American Stirling Dickinson. This and other art institutions began to attract American exchange students, and returning GIs after World War 2, who came to study and live in San Miguel. The cultural center is part of the Instituto Nacional de Bellas Artes and is usually referred to by locals as "Bellas Artes". It is a two story cloister surrounding an extremely spacious courtyard, with a large fountain in the middle. It houses art exhibits, classrooms for drawing, painting, sculpture, lithography, textiles, ceramics, dramatic arts, ballet, regional dance, piano and guitar. One hall of the old convent is dedicated to a mural by famous Mexican artist David Alfaro Siqueiros, but it was never finished. The complex also has a museum, a writers and poets venue, two art galleries, and an auditorium that hosts such events as "The International Festival of Jazz and Blues" and the "Guanajuato International Film Festival".

25. Transport Yourself At Film And Theater Venues

As a lifelong film lover I was concerned upon moving to San Miguel that I might miss the great playhouses and movie theaters to which I had grown accustomed in San Francisco and New York. The only big screen movie house is up on the hill above town, in the only (very small) mall in the San Miguel area. However, I need not have worried. There are four venues in Centro that regularly show films: Cine Bacco, the Pocket Theaters, the Shelter Theater, and the Santa Ana Theater. All but the Santa Ana provide alcoholic drinks and popcorn with the 100 peso ($5.00 U.S.) price of admission. In addition, two of the premier venues in town, the Angela Peralta Opera House and the Bellas Artes theater, host the annual "Guanajuato International Film Festival", 10 days of free films from all over the world. Live play productions are hosted throughout the year by the San Miguel Playhouse, St. Paul's Church, the Shelter Theater, and the Santa Ana Theater. San Miguel has also been a choice locale to use as a backdrop for the production of films and television programs. Both Mexican and foreign productions have been shot here, many of which feature gunfights by mustached protagonists. Projects that have been filmed here include *"Once Upon a Time in Mexico"*, with Antonio Banderas, Salma Hayek, and Johnny Depp, a television biopic of *Francisco "Pancho" Villa*, and *"The Mask of Zorro II"*.

26. Create Anew At International Writers' Conference

I have attended the San Miguel Writers' Conference & Literary Festival both of the years I have lived in San Miguel and have thoroughly enjoyed all aspects of my experience. It is quite impressive that a conference of this size and stature can succeed in a place as small, and some would say remote, as San Miguel. As the largest and most prestigious co-cultural, bi-lingual literary gathering in the Americas, each February the Conference attracts distinguished authors, established and emerging writers, industry experts, teaching professionals, and avid readers from the United States, Canada, Mexico, and Europe. In addition to the 750 participants in craft and commerce workshops and 12 master classes, another 10,000 or so seats are filled during the Conference at the main stage ballroom events, which include keynote presentations, expert panels, and seminars. A newer event at the conference, closing it in style on Sunday afternoon after five days, is the Storytellers event. Great and inspiring stories each year. I hope to participate in it myself one time soon.

27. Quaff Tequila And Mescal: Cantina Tour Anyone?

A singular San Miguel experience is taking the Cantina Trolley Tour
to four very old and original Mexican cantinas. In rural Mexico,
a cantina traditionally is a type of bar frequented by males for
drinking alcohol and eating *botanas* (appetizers). Cantinas can often
be distinguished by signs that expressly prohibit entrance to women
and minors. Some of the traditional restrictions on entry to cantinas
are beginning to fade away. However, in many areas it is still viewed
as scandalous for proper ladies to be seen visiting a genuine cantina.
Ladies are always more than welcome on the Cantina Trolley Tour,
and are often celebrated for their presence in the San Miguel
cantinas. The trolleys themselves remind me of the San Francisco
cable cars and trolleys, the ones on wheels, as opposed to the
original ones that run on tracks. Anyone who drinks alcohol is
required to try the tequila and mescal when you are visiting San
Miguel. After all, they are the national drinks, and the only "real"
mescals and tequilas come from Mexico. Now that they have become
a high-priced, high-end drink, with tequila bars appearing all over
the world, what better place to experience that unique type of high,
and fun, than in an authentic Mexican cantina. All around the historic
center there are over 80 bars and cantinas, as well as various
nightclubs. Many of the cantinas have the swinging double doors,
like those seen in Old West movies, which is very appropriate since
in some ways going to San Miguel is like taking a trip back to the Old
West .

28. Belt Out And Boogie: Live Music And Dancing

For a town of only 100,000 people San Miguel has far more than its share of things to do at night, every night of the week all year round. For those who love Latin dancing, especially salsa and cumbia, two clubs with live bands and lively dance floors are La Chula and Hacienda. If you want to learn these dances, or improve your moves, there are a number of private and group classes. The most favored teacher among my circle of friends is Fernando, who teaches private lessons at a studio at his home, and group lessons at a much larger studio around the corner. Listening and dancing to a variety of other live bands, and different genres of music, takes place regularly at such well-established and popular clubs and restaurants as Paprika, Mama Mia's, Cent'anni, and Santos, a late night club where all ages go to dance their asses off to American and British rock 'n' roll, played by outstanding Mexican rock and blues musicians. Those who love to take a microphone into their hand and live their rock 'n' roll fantasy, or who prefer to play back-up singers and sing along, will always find a festive and fun crowd for Karaoke at The Beer Company.

29. Ascend To The Stars: Rooftops

One of the most pleasurable aspects of life here is sitting on the roofs that almost every home, restaurant, and bar in San Miguel has for enjoying the dazzling views, mountain air, and exotic sunsets. I already have so many magnificent memories of rooftop meals, drinks, dancing, parties, and just sitting around with friends hanging out and talking. One of my treasured recollections is from New Year's Eve 2016/2017. A group of friends were sitting on the roof at one of our homes, relaxing, drinking wine, enjoying the sunset, the night sky, and the fireworks going off all around our 360 degree view, when someone suggested that we take turns sharing what we are grateful for about the past year and our lives here in San Miguel. Since each of us had begun a new life in San Miguel, from the U.S., Europe, and other parts of Mexico, we were all able to talk about what it meant to take a big leap, in most cases leaving behind family, friends, and our former life, and move to another world, a place we knew little about before moving here, but trusted our intuition, a lifetime of experience of living and traveling the world, and faith that San Miguel de Allende was indeed an extraordinary and magical place. For me, it was one of the nicest New Year's Eves I have ever spent. I think my friends may have felt the same way.

30. Celebrate: Weddings And Receptions Galore

If you are looking for an uncommon and genuinely romantic place to hold a wedding and reception I don't think you can find too many places in the world to match San Miguel. The combination of old world charm, in this 16th - 18th century colonial Latin city in the mountains, modern conveniences, and a place where romance and adventure always seem to be in the air, these are just a few of the reasons that I have seen more weddings taking place in San Miguel than I have ever seen anywhere else. The city's many charming hotels, restaurants, churches, musicians, and event spaces seem able to have something to offer weddings of any size and budget. If you have the money to afford a high-end wedding, the ones I have seen with the wedding taking place at the Parroquia, and the reception at the world class Rosewood Hotel, look like something out of a big budget Hollywood film.

"Mexicans know that a party has been outstandingly successful if at the end of it there are at least a couple of clusters of longtime or first-time acquaintances leaning on each other against a wall, sobbing helplessly."

Alma Guillermoprieto

("Serenading the Future")

31. Ponder Spirituality: Tales Of Catholics and Pagans

You will have an assortment of church tours from which to choose in San Miguel. Partly because there are very many churches in our city. In fact in a city of only approximately 100,000 people, there are over 400 churches! The two tours that I am most familiar with, because I have taken them, are the *Historical Walking Tours* (which covers more than just the churches), given by volunteers for *Patronato Pro Niños*, an NGO that provides disadvantaged children with free dental and medical benefits, and Joseph Toone's *Historical and Culture Walking Tour*. His tour tells the secrets and stories behind many of the church art and symbols, and behind the fiestas and spiritual celebrations that take place all through the year. It is a primer for San Miguel de Allende's more unique traditions and celebrations, which are an extraordinary mixture of an ancestral pagan past and the Catholic faith.

32. Party Down: 322 Fiesta Days Each Year!

Most of the festivals here are purely Mexican, combining social activity with religious expression. Throughout the year there are pilgrimages, all-night vigils, ringing church bells, parades, processions, and fireworks. The largest celebration of the year is that of the town's patron saint, the Archangel Michael. The angel's feast day is the 29th of September, but festivities take place for an entire week. I had been told that September, the last month that I lived here during my first year, since I moved here in early October, was the biggest party month of all. This was difficult to believe, since each of the previous 11 months had seemed like the biggest party month. So when the week or two of hoopla surrounding September 16, Mexico's Independence Day, was over, I naively thought that I could chill out for the rest of September. Nope. I had not been warned that although Independence Day was the biggest national holiday of the year, the celebration of Michael the Archangel was the biggest local holiday of the year. And in a town that only has 43 days per year when some religious or secular holiday is not being celebrated, that is saying an awful lot, to be the biggest fiesta among 322 fiesta days a year!

33. Feel Semana Santa: Holy Week In San Miguel

You will find out, if you come during this week, that to experience Semana Santa in San Miguel de Allende is to feel the full force of Mexico's Catholic heritage, and the deep hold it has on the hearts of her people. This is the most awe-inspiring time to visit San Miguel. All over Mexico, Holy Week and Easter are celebrated as significant religious holidays. Processions, altars and "Passion Plays" reenacting the last days of Christ are performed in various cities. Nowhere in Mexico is Semana Santa recognized with such reverence, tradition, and awe as in San Miguel de Allende. Visitors both devout and curious come from all over Mexico and the world to experience the intense emotion of these observances of the Passion and the Resurrection of Christ. Despite the crowds, this is not a tourist show. These Holy Week ceremonies are deeply felt statements of faith. Many of the rituals go back centuries. It is a privilege to be allowed to observe them, and even to participate, if your faith leads you to do so. In San Miguel, Semana Santa, or Holy Week, is not really a "week." The pageantry leading up to the celebration of the Resurrection of Christ on Easter Sunday actually begins two weeks before Easter and continues into the week after.

34. Get Crazy: Day Of The Locos!

Mexicans never seem to need a reason to celebrate or throw a party, and do not seem to ever shy away from an occasion to dress up. One of the local traditions that I find especially endearing is the "Day of the Locos (Crazies)!", an only-in-San Miguel fiesta. It takes place in mid-June on the Sunday closest to June 13, since it is related to San Antonio, the saint you ask to find anything you have lost. There is a big parade around town and people of all ages dress up in whatever crazy costumes they wish to express themselves in that day. There are some elements similar to Halloween, where you will see current events played out, like the number of Trump and Hilary masks seen in 2016 during the primary season. But it is also reminiscent of Mardi Gras, with candies and other items being thrown by the parade participants out to the crowd. Like so many other festivities in San Miguel there are deep religious roots behind the celebration. My favorite part is seeing all of the Mexican macho men dressed up as women, playing their cross-dressing role to the hilt.

35. Bring Back The Dead: Dia De Los Muertos

My most cherished holiday each year, in a city and country that celebrates more holidays, with more fiestas and fireworks, than anywhere else in the world, is Dia de los Muertos, the Day of the Dead. Even though I have only lived here for a year and a half, I feel like I have already been through three Day of the Dead celebrations, although one was in the month of March, and turned out to be the Day of the Dead sets in Mexico City for the 2015 James Bond film "Spectre"! The timing coincides with Halloween in the United States, but the main day is, rather than October 31, November 2. However, the celebrations usually last about a week. With so many expats living in San Miguel, Halloween has gotten rolled into the Day of the Dead festivities, even, especially, among the Mexican families and their children. But I prefer the purely Mexican part of the holiday, with the Calacas (skull figures), Catrinas (dressed up female skeletons), Mojigangas (giant puppets), parades, fiestas, and fireworks, every day and night. Most unique is the way the spirits of the dead are invited back to share food, drink, and partying with their family and friends. Altars are built in each home to honor those who have passed on. I have made my own altars in my bedroom during the past two Day of the Dead weeks, to honor my mother and father, each of whom passed away not long before I moved to Mexico. In the Mexican tradition I placed chocolate and movie star memories on my Mom's side, and beer and baseball memories on my Dad's side. The Mexican families celebrate and honor outside the home as well, spending often all day at the local cemetery, with flowers, food, drink, music, and song, hanging out with the spirits of their loved ones.

36. Shoot Hoops: Parque Juarez

South of the historic center, down Aldama, the street that runs directly behind the Parroquia, is Parque Juárez. This park was established at the beginning of the 20th century on the banks of a river in a French park style, with gardens, fountains, decorative pools, wrought iron benches, old bridges, and footpaths. There is an area for children with a playground and two basketball courts, which host lively games for males and females of all age groups. Being the largest city park in town it has also hosted big music and food events, Day of the Dead memorial installations, and the recent International Women's Day marches and speeches.

37. Journey Down The Ancha

When I first arrived here I would hear people talk about "going to the Ancha", or "walking the Ancha", or "it's on the Ancha", and wonder what the heck they were talking about. I soon learned that there was a street called Ancha de San Antonio and that, because there was another street named San Antonio Abad, everyone called one of the main commercial streets and arteries in and out of San Miguel "The Ancha". I can go out on the Ancha on any given day of the week to do my organic food shopping, visit several different types of pharmacies, buy my wines and champagnes from all over the world, have breakfast at Café Monet, lunch at Hecho en Mexico, and dinner at Antigua Trattoria, and finish the day with music and a beer at The Beer Company or Paprika.

38. Reconnect: El Charco And Full Moon Ceremonies

The Botanical Gardens of San Miguel, formally known as *El Charco del Ingenio,* is located in the hills above town. It is an ecological reserve, dedicated to the restoration and preservation of Mexican flora, and it propagates species in danger of extinction. The reserve is centered on a canyon, at the bottom of which is a fresh spring which forms a natural pool. The canyon was the center of a number of myths and legends during the pre-Hispanic period. There are also the remains of a colonial era aqueduct and other waterworks on the property. But there are three memorable things I have done at *El Charco* that go beyond the beautiful natural setting. One is the monthly Full Moon Ceremony, led by native elders, who lead the gathered "tribe" in calling in the directions and blessing the land, animals, spirits, and people. A second special event is the annual music celebration "Music on the Rocks", a fundraiser that takes place in March each year. But the most extraordinary thing I have experienced there is the Murmuration, which you can read about in the next chapter.

39. Be In Awe: The Murmuration

There are few scenes in nature that I have witnessed any more stunning for the mind, body, and soul than The Murmuration. My daughter is a biologist and environmental consultant, so when she visited me in San Miguel I told her we need to do everything we can to try to go up to the reservoir near *El Charco*, the Botanical Gardens, and see if we can catch The Murmuration. I had only seen a video of it, but a friend of mine is married to the President of the only chapter of the Audubon Society in Mexico, here in San Miguel, and he had told me about tours she leads to see it. We were not able to go on one of the tours, so we ventured out on our own in a taxi. The guide at *El Charco* told us that the best place to see The Murmuration was to drive further south to the other side of the reservoir. The taxi driver must have been new, because he did not seem to know his way around, but I encouraged him to take the dirt road south, and to ask some hikers where to go next. We got as close as we could by car and walked the rest of the way towards the water. It was dusk, the time it happens, and it had started to drizzle. But we were determined, and were well rewarded when a flock of many hundreds, if not thousands, of small starlings appeared and started flying in spiraling, artistic, and spiritual-looking patterns, constantly shifting, growing as many stragglers joined the rest, shrinking as sections broke off to form other, smaller Murmurations over an island of trees in the reservoir. If you ever get the chance to see one you should do what you can to experience the totally unique Murmuration in person.

40. Delight In The Monarch Butterfly Migration

I had heard that the monarch butterfly migration that takes place in the state of Michoacan, less than a two hour drive from San Miguel, is a must see wonder of the natural world. It happens from October through March each year. I had been to the monarch migrations in Pacific Grove, California, near Monterey, in the past, and they were quite impressive. I recently learned from a Conservation Biologist, who has been to both places, that about 20,000 monarch butterflies migrate to Pacific Grove annually, whereas at its peak in 2000 there were over 1 billion *Mariposa Monarcas* in Michoacan! He has been going there for the past 30 years and told me that the best time to see them is in the last week of February and the first week in March. I will be there in 2018!

"We travel, some of us forever, to seek other places, other lives, other souls."

Anais Nin

41. Serenade Your Spirit: Mariachis

Some of the most beloved characters and sights of San Miguel are the ubiquitous mariachi players. They travel all around town, in their many-colored traditional Mexican outfits (all of the players in each band dress in the same colors, but the colors of each band vary), playing traditional Mexican music beloved by Mexicans of all ages. They can be seen serenading couples in restaurants, playing at the bandstand in the Jardin, in parades, wedding processions, around the giant mojigangas, hanging out around the Parroquia, and, for big fiesta weekends, five or more groups of them all playing in the same general area.

Unlike some expats, I never get tired of hearing the mariachi bands play, because it always represents to me a celebration or important occasion of one sort or another, even if beloved sad songs are being played. And if your only experience with mariachis is from watching the "El Mariachi" trilogy, with Antonio Banderas and Salma Hayek, these guys are not exactly like that. I have never seen them armed, or being chased by the authorities, or by banditos!

42. Salsa With A Mojiganga

Mojiganga was not a word I had ever heard in my previous world travels. But once in San Miguel I quickly became familiar with seeing them in parades, fiestas, wedding celebrations, outside a new store or restaurant, and just walking around the streets of San Miguel. Once you see one you quickly realize that they are like nothing you have ever encountered before. A Mojiganga (pronounced: mo-he-gang-ga) is a giant puppet that is also used as a sculpture or a grand scale design element for a large event. The head and bust are made of papier mâché, which is then mounted on a tall supporting A-frame structure. The giant costume is then "worn" by people who are usually surprisingly small inside them, peering out through a little opening, so they can see where they are going. They range from approximately 6 to 18 feet tall (2-6 meters). The giant dancing puppets seem to always be joyous and are often an essential part of San Miguel fiestas. During wedding festivities you will often see a female and male Mojiganga together, representing the bride and groom.

43. Light The Sky: Fuegos Artificiales

Ever since I was a kid growing up in New Jersey I have always loved watching fireworks. That thrill has never diminished during my adult life, when I would go out of my way to see fireworks in the New York harbor, over San Francisco Bay, and during my world travels. But I cannot believe there could be another place on this planet (with the possible exception of Disneyland and Disney World!) with more fireworks per week, month, or year than San Miguel de Allende, Mexico. I have already said that there are only 43 days per year when there is not some sort of fiesta or holiday, and every one of them comes with *fuegos artificiales,* fireworks, any time of day or night. In fact many of them go off between the hours of 4:00 – 6:00 AM, not my favorite time of day. But the majority are still set off during prime time night time hours. They can go on for hours, and are a sight to behold. Especially when they appear over the night sky in front of the spectacular Parroquia cathedral, or when you can see multiple fireworks shows at once from rooftops around town. But unlike pyrotechnic displays in most places, which tend to be set off in one central location, the *fuegos artificiales* in San Miguel can go off anywhere at any time. Just in the last two nights they could be seen clearly, close by, from my *terraza* outside my home, even though I live in a quiet neighborhood away from any central location.

44. Travel Out Of Your Comfort Zone: Is Mexico Safe?

The biggest question on the minds of Americans considering traveling to Mexico, especially to anywhere beyond the "made for Americans and Canadians" coastal beach towns, is "Is it safe to go there?" I rarely hear those concerns from experienced world travelers, who have traveled to anywhere off of the "first world" track, especially to parts of Asia, Africa, or Latin America. But given the very skewed U.S. mainstream media, whose number one goal is to sell advertising, and therefore to attract viewers through the most sensational news stories, Mexico has been given a very bad rap over the years. What I, and all of my expat friends who live in Mexico, tell people is, it is no different than traveling in the U.S: If you don't go to places you shouldn't go to, at times you shouldn't be there, especially by yourself, you will be fine. In a year and a half of living in San Miguel, and traveling all around Mexico, often by myself, I have never once felt threatened or unsafe.

45. View Mexico's Sistine Chapel: Atotonilco

Atotonilco, a small community outside San Miguel, is best known for its religious sanctuary, a church complex which has World Heritage Site status, along with the historic center of San Miguel. The complex was built in the 18th century by Father Luis Felipe Neri de Alfaro, who, according to tradition, was called upon by a vision of Jesus with a crown of thorns on his head and carrying a cross. The main feature of the complex is the rich Mexican Baroque mural work that adorns the main nave and chapels. The mural work has led the complex to be dubbed the "Sistine Chapel of Mexico." The most interesting story about Atotonilco to many foreigners, however, is not the Sistine Chapel comparisons, or the fact that the Virgin of Guadalupe banner for the hastily recruited army, at the start of the revolution against Spain, was taken from here on September 16, 1810, but rather the tales of flagellation. As far back as the days of the early Spanish conquest people have come from all over to do penance here and to atone for their sins. It is common even today to see a line of pilgrims not only walking many miles, but even crawling for long distances, sometimes carrying heavy crosses. It has been said that you can even buy whips for self-flagellation at Atotonilco. Reminds me of the Opus Dei scenes in "The DaVinci Code". If you wish to counterbalance your Catholic guilt after that visit, a spiritual visit of a different type can be experienced nearby at the Galleria Atotonilco, located in two beautiful buildings and housing what is called the best Mexican folk art collection in the world.

46. Sooth Your Body: Hot Springs, Pools, And Spas

You will find when you visit that the area has become a popular destination for health and healing. San Miguel has a number of natural hot springs resorts for day visits or longer stays. La Gruta, where I have taken family and friends for relaxing days in the sun, has three separate outdoor thermal pools. A dome-topped thermal pool leads off of the warmest pool. To get there bathers venture through a water tunnel before reaching the "waterfall" cascades, which blast down from above several times an hour. Another popular hot springs location is Escondido Place, loved by many San Miguelense (residents of San Miguel). It contains beautiful grass covered grounds and walking paths, ponds, three enclosed warm pools and several cooler pools outdoors. San Miguel also has more than its share of healing centers. The one I am most familiar with is Lifepath, which offers yoga and meditation classes, massage, and many varieties of alternative healing methodologies and healers. They also have rooms where retreat attendees can stay for up to a week or more. Treatments for the body, mind, and spirit can be found throughout San Miguel, including the spas, swimming pools, and hot tubs at major hotels in town like the Rosewood, La Aldea, *Misión, and* Real de Minas. All have health facilities in beautiful outdoor settings, with spas and swimming pools that can be used year round, in the almost always pleasant climate in San Miguel.

47. Ride 'Em: Horseback Riding At Cañada De La Virgen

When my daughter from San Francisco and brother, sister-in-law, and two nieces from New York came to visit me in San Miguel we were looking for some things to do outside of the city, to get out into the country and experience some of the nature and Mexican culture in the small villages in the *campo*. I knew there were a number of places where you can go horseback riding outside of San Miguel. A friend recommended one run by an American expat, who works together with the local Mexicans of the region, near Cañada de la Virgen, an Otomi archaeological site that was first discovered in 1998. She and three Mexican guides took us out riding for hours in the mountains, desert, and canyons, overlooking a river deep in the canyon. Not only were the views breathtaking, but the best part for me, having grown up horseback riding in the Catskill Mountains of New York, was that I got to take off trotting and galloping as fast as I wanted to go, something that has become very rare to find in the U.S. anymore due to insurance concerns. After we got back to the ranch we were treated to a delicious home-cooked Mexican meal, with refreshing fruit drinks and cold cervezas, and tequila for anyone brave enough to take a shot in the middle of the afternoon!

48. Climb To The Top: Ancient Pyramids

The two greatest ancient pyramid sites in Mexico are Teotihuacán, located outside of Mexico City, and Chichen Itza, in the upper northeastern section of Mexico, on the Yucatan Peninsula. With its famous Pyramid of the Sun and Pyramid of the Moon, Teotihuacan was the epicenter of Mesoamerica, dating back to the first two centuries B.C. It flourished until its collapse sometime around A.D. 700.

Chichen Itza is the most popular of the Mayan ruins, and dates from around A.D. 600-1200 . But what I did not know when I moved to San Miguel is that the state of Guanajuato, and its close neighboring state of Queretaro, have many of their own ancient pyramids. One just has to talk to the locals to find out where they are and which are the most interesting to visit.

49. Explore Mesoamerica: Coffee (Albert) Tours

There are many travel and tour companies in San Miguel and the surrounding area catering to the large number of tourists and other visitors each year. If you are looking for high quality, unique tours, especially for people who are interested in history, archeology, anthropology, and the type of information you will not find on a website, most people agree that the best way to go is to take a tour led by Albert Coffee. A bilingual archeologist from the U.S., who worked on the 2004 excavation at Cañada de la Virgen, the archaeological zone located just 15 minutes southwest of San Miguel de Allende, Albert has now guided more than 6,000 visitors on the tours he has been leading since 2011.

Cañada de la Virgen is his local specialty, but he leads a wide spectrum of expeditions, both in the areas near to San Miguel, as well as all over Mexico, to the most compelling and magnificent places such as Oaxaca, Chiapas, Teotihuacan, Chichen Itzá, Monte Albán and many more.

50. Take A Magic Carpet Ride: Magic Towns

If you have some extra time there are many compelling day trips that can be explored within short drives from San Miguel. A superb one, just an hour or less drive to the west, is the state capital city of Guanajuato. It, like most cities in the state, dates back to colonial times. Entering and exiting the city you drive through a maze of beguiling underground tunnels, a remnant of a long-ago effort to avoid flooding when Guanajuato was a thriving mining town. Guanajuato also hosts the world famous Festival Internacional Cervantino for three weeks every October, one of the most important international artistic and cultural events in Mexico and *Latin America*, and one of four major events of its type in the world. About a 30 minute drive south from San Miguel takes you to Queretaro, a thriving city of about 800,000, one of the fastest growing in Mexico.

Queretaro has a charming colonial center. Just outside the town are short trips to a pyramid and to the village of Bernal, known for its enormous monolith of massive rock, the **Peña de Bernal**, the third highest on the planet. Recently, the town of Bernal acquired the title of **Pueblo Mágico** ("Magic Town"). The Magic Towns in Mexico are designated for being localities that have magic symbolic attributes, legends, or history. Pozos, only a 30 minute drive from San Miguel, once known throughout colonial Mexico for its opulence and its thriving mining industry, has been a virtual ghost town for almost a century. It is currently experiencing a resurgence of interest on the part of visitors looking for an uncommon adventure. Pozos is now *also officially* a **Pueblo Mágico** in Mexico. Nearby Dolores Hidalgo is known primarily for its *ceramics* industry, started by Father Hidalgo, *who* uttered his famous cry for the independence of Mexico ("La **Grito**") there in the early hours of September 16, 1810.

> TOURIST

GREATER THAN A TOURIST

Visit GreaterThanATourist.com
http://GreaterThanATourist.com

Sign up for the Greater Than a Tourist Newsletter
http://eepurl.com/cxspyf

Follow us on Facebook:
https://www.facebook.com/GreaterThanATourist

Follow us on Pinterest:
http://pinterest.com/GreaterThanATourist

Follow us on Instagram:
http://Instagram.com/GreaterThanATourist

> TOURIST

GREATER THAN A TOURIST

Please leave your honest review of this book on Amazon and Goodreads. Thank you.

We appreciate your positive and negative feedback as we try to provide tourist guidance in their next trip from a local.

> TOURIST

GREATER THAN A TOURIST

You can find Greater Than a Tourist books on Amazon.

> TOURIST

GREATER THAN A TOURIST

WHERE WILL YOU TRAVEL TO NEXT?

> TOURIST

GREATER THAN A TOURIST

Our Story

Traveling is a passion of this series creator. She studied abroad in college, and for their honeymoon Lisa and her husband toured Europe. During her travels to Malta, an older man tried to give her some advice based on his own experience living on the island since he was a young boy. She thought he was just trying to sell her something. When traveling to some places she was wary to talk to locals because she was afraid that they weren't being genuine. She created this book series to give you as a tourist an inside view on the place you are exploring and the ability to learn what locals would like to tell tourist.   A topic that they are very passionate about.

> TOURIST

GREATER THAN A TOURIST

Notes

Made in the USA
San Bernardino, CA
05 July 2018